Head of Blind-worm. $\frac{1}{2}$

A Book=scorpion (*Chelifer cancroides*). $\frac{5}{1}$

a
Cotton=stainer

Epeiridæ.

a, male, and *b*, female, of *Epeira stellata; c*, characteristic orb=web of an epeirid (*Epeira strix*).

The Dr Drago (*Drac* eatus)

Click-beetle, natural size.

Proxys punctulatus.

Parasite of the Beaver (*Platypsyllus castoris*). (Line shows natural size.)

Agonoderus dorsalis (Le Conte). Vertical line shows natural size.

Hawthorn-tingis *arcuata*), one of the enlarged about ten ti

Hellgrammite (*a*) and Hellgrammite=fly.

The Twig=girdler (*Oncideres cingulata*). $\frac{1}{1}$
a, a branch girdled by the beetle.

Sinea diadema, one of the *Reduviidæ.* (Line shows natural size.)

The Bait=bug.

Rose-beetle (*Cetonia aurata*). Vertical line shows natural size.

Flour-beetle (*Ter litor*). (Line show size.)

Galeruca notata

Ground-beetle (*Caloso calidum*), natural size.

Eurygaster alternatus; wings partly open. (Line shows natural size.)

A Species of *Phrynus*, about life-size.

Spiderwort Owlet-moth (*Prodenia flavimedia*). *a*, larva; *b*, wings of moth.

Thighed Metapodius (*Metapodius femoratus*).

The Cucujo.

Ephemeridæ. European May-fly (*Eph. vulgata*) and its sub-larva.

Bombardier-beetle (*Brachinus stygicornis*). (Vertical line shows natural size.)

Podisus placidus. *a*, enlarged; *b*, natural size.

Libellulidæ. Development of a dragon-fly, showing the subaquatic larva, emergence from the pupa, and the adult fully winged insect.

A Flea (*Pulex irritans*). *a*, puncturing stylets of the proboscis.

A Bristletail (*Lepisma saccharina*). $^{5}/_{1}$

Phymata erosa.

Atypus sulzeri. (Vertical line shows natural size.)

Grape-vine Fidia (*F. viticida*). (Line shows natural size.)

Bacon-beetle.

spider

spid

er

by

Ting Morris

illustrated by

Desiderio Sanzi

designed by

Deb Miner

A⁺

SMART APPLE MEDIA

You are the first one up this morning … or so you think.

You rush outside and breathe in the fresh fall air. But then, suddenly, you stop.

Look at that amazing construction right in front of you! Its threads are so fine they are almost invisible. You nearly walked into this beautiful silken trap. But who made it, and where's the builder?

Turn the page and take a closer look.

ARACHNIDS

Spiders belong to an animal family called arachnids, which also includes scorpions, mites, and ticks. They are not insects. Spiders have eight legs, while ants, bees, butterflies, and other insects have six.

LITTLE SOFTIES

A spider has no bones. A hard skin or outer skeleton protects its body like a suit of armor. When the spider grows, it cracks open the old skin, and a new skin underneath takes its place. This is called molting.

The expert weaver is a garden spider.

You must have interrupted her in the middle of her work. She holds a strand of silk on which she can swing to the web or away from it at the slightest movement. This helps her avoid danger.

Now she's come out of hiding to continue making the spirals. She's in a hurry to finish the web so she can catch her breakfast.

WORLD OF SPIDERS

There are more than 30,000 different kinds of spiders, and probably many more that haven't yet been found. Spiders live everywhere, from the seashore to the highest mountains, driest deserts, and deepest caves. You'll find them in parks and woods, in holes in the ground, under leaves, and even in your home. This spider is a garden spider. Have you noticed the cross pattern on its back? It's also called a cross spider.

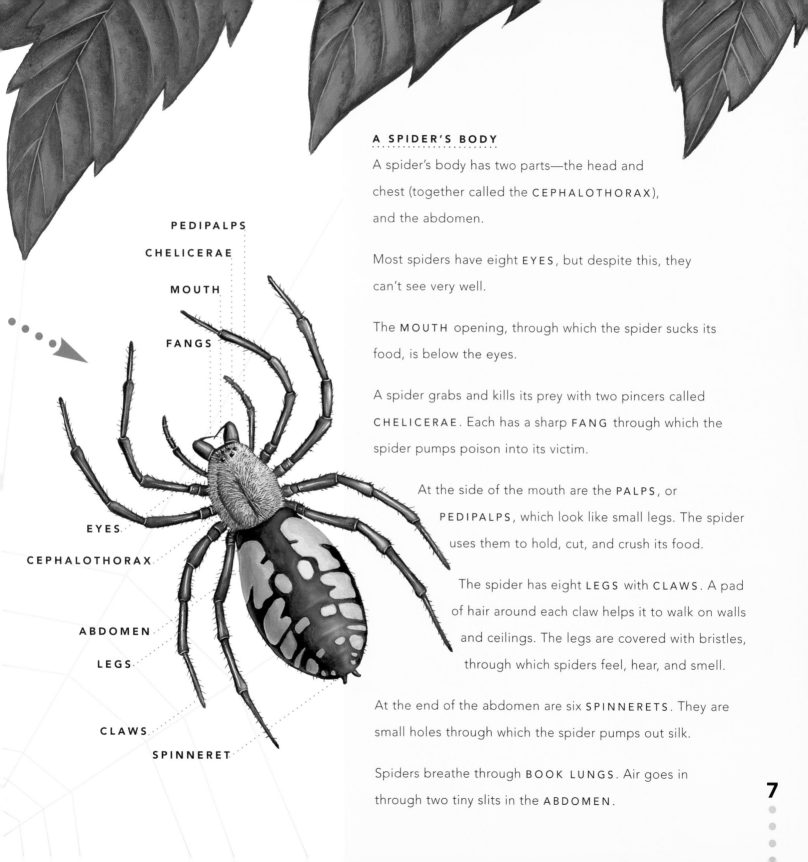

PEDIPALPS
CHELICERAE
MOUTH
FANGS
EYES
CEPHALOTHORAX
ABDOMEN
LEGS
CLAWS
SPINNERET

A SPIDER'S BODY

A spider's body has two parts—the head and chest (together called the CEPHALOTHORAX), and the abdomen.

Most spiders have eight EYES, but despite this, they can't see very well.

The MOUTH opening, through which the spider sucks its food, is below the eyes.

A spider grabs and kills its prey with two pincers called CHELICERAE. Each has a sharp FANG through which the spider pumps poison into its victim.

At the side of the mouth are the PALPS, or PEDIPALPS, which look like small legs. The spider uses them to hold, cut, and crush its food.

The spider has eight LEGS with CLAWS. A pad of hair around each claw helps it to walk on walls and ceilings. The legs are covered with bristles, through which spiders feel, hear, and smell.

At the end of the abdomen are six SPINNERETS. They are small holes through which the spider pumps out silk.

Spiders breathe through BOOK LUNGS. Air goes in through two tiny slits in the ABDOMEN.

The spider is a fast worker. It's taken her less than an hour to spin this web. But she's had a lot of practice. When an insect is caught, it usually damages the web, so the spider spins a new one almost every night.

This garden spider is laying down the last spiral of sticky silk. Can you see the silk coming out of her body? She's putting it in place with her legs. It won't be long before something gets caught in her sticky trap. Fortunately for her, she's got oily feet and never gets stuck herself.

LIFELINE

Not all spiders spin webs, but they all
need silk. Wherever a spider goes, it spins
a silk dragline behind itself. If it senses
danger, it drops down to the ground and
hides or hangs in the air until the enemy
is gone. This lifeline also comes in handy
for swinging down from high places and
traveling through the air.

SILK SUCKERS

Spiders spin tiny disks of
sticky threads and attach
them to walls, trees, and
other surfaces. These
suckers hold the spider's
dragline and web in place.

The garden spider has been waiting patiently for food to arrive. The tiny glue drops sparkle in the early morning sun, making the silk threads look beautiful—but not to these small insects! They have come to a very sticky end.

The spider can feel that something big and tasty has flown into her web. It's struggling to get out and has broken part of the web, but the sticky silk is very strong.

It's time for the spider to rush over and see what she has caught.

BUILDING INSTRUCTIONS FOR GARDEN SPIDERS

Spin a bridge line between two twigs. Strengthen the first thread and spin a new one that hangs loosely below it.

Go to the middle of the second thread, drop down, and fasten a third thread in place with a sticky sucker. This is your Y-shaped framework. The fork in the Y will be the middle of your web.

Spin bottom and side threads to finish the framework. Add threads like the spokes of a wheel. Make sure the spokes meet in the middle of the Y.

Make a small spiral in the middle to lock the spokes in place.

Build scaffolding by spinning a spiral from the middle to the edge of the web.

When you have reached the edge, turn back toward the middle. Lay down the sticky spiral used to trap insects. Eat up the scaffolding along the way.

NO WASTE
The garden spider eats its old web before making a new one, so nothing is wasted.

The spider has caught a big fly. It was buzzing and squirming madly before she rushed across the web and stabbed it with her deadly fangs. Poison flowed into the wound until the fly could no longer move.

It's silent in the web now. **The spider wraps her prey in sheets of silk, so there's no escape.** She ties it up in threads. When she's finished wrapping, she'll get on with the dinner preparations. First she'll spray the fly with saliva and wait for it to go soft.

SLEEPY HAMMOCK

The money spider hangs under its hammock web in the bushes and waits for flying insects, especially aphids, to get trapped in the criss-crossed threads.

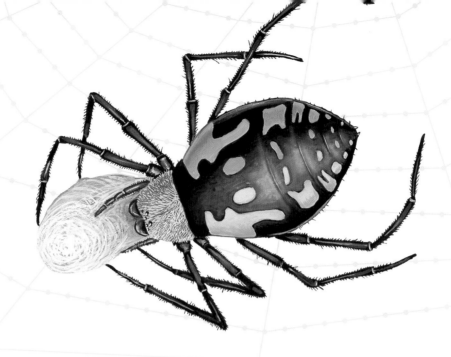

LIQUID DIET

A spider's mouth is too small to eat solids, so it sprays food with saliva to make it soft enough to suck up. It leaves the hard outside skeleton. The next time you see a garden spider's web, look underneath it. You can tell what the owner has eaten by its leftovers: the hard outer bodies of flies, mosquitoes, wasps, and even other spiders.

FIERCE HUNTER

The wolf spider is an excellent hunter. Unlike its web-spinning cousins, it has good vision. It simply creeps up on its victim and pounces.

DOWN UNDER

The Australian funnel-web spider hides at the bottom of a silk funnel in tall grass or under a rock. Its web spreads out across the ground in a messy tangle of threads to catch jumping insects. The funnel-web spider has sharp fangs and a fierce bite.

A garden spider's work is never done. After her meal, she has to repair the web for a new catch. **But suddenly she feels a thread moving.** Could this be another victim, or is it an enemy? The spider gets ready to attack.

When the stranger pulls on her web again, she recognizes the signal. It's a male garden spider who wants to be her mate. She needs his sperm for her eggs, so she goes to meet him.

WEDDING PRESENT

The male nursery web spider captures a fly, wraps it in silk, and offers it as a present to his larger mate. That way she won't eat him!

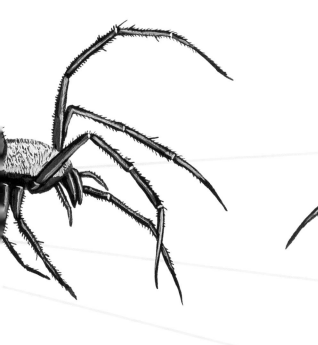

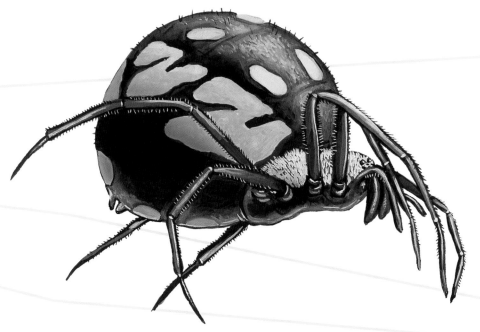

WHEN TWO SPIDERS MEET

Male spiders are much smaller than females and have to be very careful. When a male spider wants to mate with a female, he makes it clear that he is not something to eat by pulling on her web in a special way. If she still attacks, he quickly drops away on his lifeline.

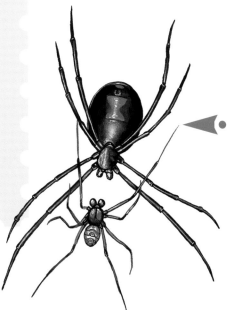

SHOWMEN

The wolf spider and other hunting spiders do a special dance to attract a partner.

BLACK WIDOWS

The male partner of a black widow spider has to be extra careful. She sometimes eats him after mating.

It's late fall, and the spider is heavy with the eggs that are swelling inside her. She is ready to lay them. She takes great care over this important job. **First she spins a saucer of silk and glues it to a gap in the tree bark.** Then she puts the eggs in the middle and covers them with liquid silk, which holds them together like seeds in a tomato. She spins a lid of fine threads over the egg saucer and wraps it up in a silk bag known as an egg sac.

The mother spider knows that her eggs will be safe throughout the winter. She will soon die.

Garden spiders never see their babies.

CARRY US! Some spider mothers carry their eggs wherever they go. Others guard the egg sac until they die in the fall. The following spring, the mother's dead body is the baby spiders' first source of food.

HOW MANY EGGS?

The number of eggs
spiders lay depends
on their size. Most
spiders lay about 100.
The smallest spiders
lay only two eggs at
a time. A big garden
spider can lay up to
1,000 eggs.

UNDERWATER HOMES

Male and female water spiders spin
silk diving bells and attach them to
water weeds. Breathing is no problem
because the bells are full of air. The spiders live
inside the bells and prey on small water animals,
such as tiny crabs and insects.

EGGS IN WATER

A water spider lays between 50 and 100 eggs.
She wraps them in a silk cocoon and hangs it in
her diving bell.

It's spring now, and the eggs are hatching inside their silk bag. But the tiny baby spiders, called spiderlings, don't come out immediately. They continue growing inside the bag and wait for a warm, sunny day.

Look, there they are! **Hundreds of spiderlings are struggling out.** They all stick together in a big clump. Can you see the fine silk thread each of them is spinning? Those are their draglines, which will help them get away from their brothers and sisters. Baby spiders quickly move apart so they don't eat each other.

HAIRY!

Tarantulas are big spiders that live in hot climates. They molt more than 20 times. After the first molt, they look just like mini-tarantulas but are a different color. They turn brown as they grow.

HELP NEEDED

Nursery web spiderlings need their mother to help them out of their silk bag. She loosens the hard silk threads for them.

OLD FOR NEW

1 A few days before molting, the spider stops eating. It hangs upside down and splits the old skin.

2 The spider slips out of its old skin, head and chest first, followed by the abdomen and then the legs.

3 Then the spider hangs by a thread and stretches its new legs to get them moving.

GROWING UP

Spiderlings shed their outer skin up to 10 times as they grow. A new, larger skin appears under the skin that has become too tight. This is called molting. The first two molts happen in the egg sac.

This looks fun! **The spiderlings climb to the top of a tall plant and wait for the wind to catch their streamer of silk.** Then they are whisked into the air by the breeze. They are lifted higher and higher, floating far away like balloons.

But now there are many dangers. Birds might eat the spiderlings in mid-flight, or the spiderlings might land in water. Lucky balloonists will come down on a plant that's perfect for making their first web.

AIR AND FOOD

Young water spiderlings stay in their mother's diving bell for a couple of weeks. During that time, she supplies them with air and food.

NICE MRS. WOLF

Not all spiderlings balloon away. Baby wolf spiders climb on their mother's back. She carries them around and feeds them for a few days.

20

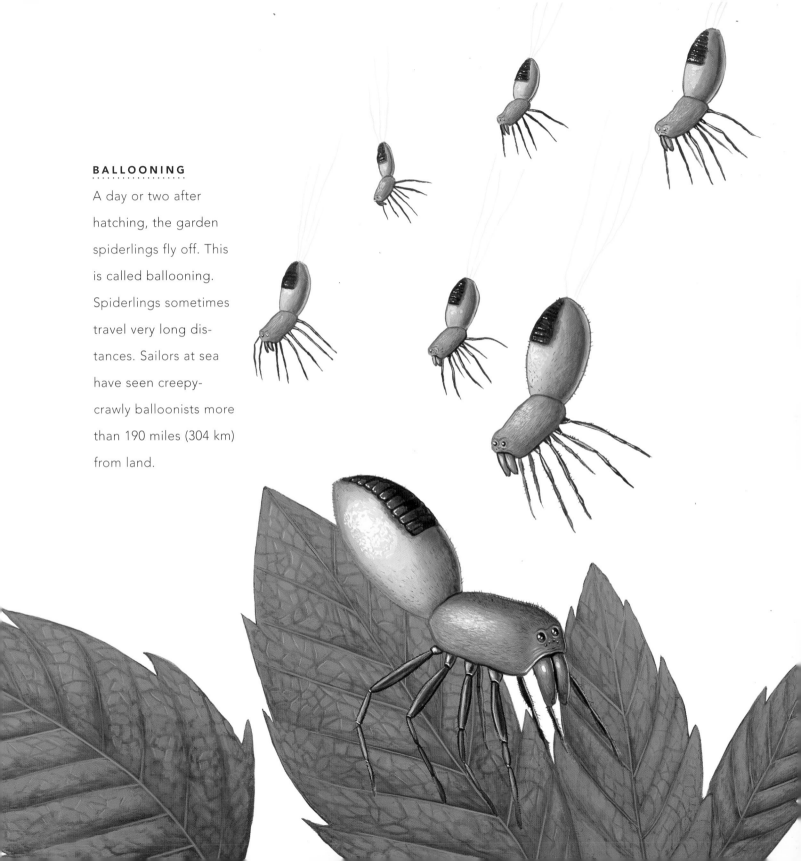

BALLOONING

A day or two after hatching, the garden spiderlings fly off. This is called ballooning. Spiderlings sometimes travel very long distances. Sailors at sea have seen creepy-crawly balloonists more than 190 miles (304 km) from land.

Most spiders are brown or gray and are difficult to see. The crab spider matches the color of the flower it hides in. It can even change color when it moves to another flower.

22

This spiderling has landed on a branch in a garden, and the first thing it does is make a web. This first web is small, but it can still catch a nice meal of insects. The spiderling hides in the grass, waiting for food. It keeps a foot on the alarm thread leading down from the web, so nothing escapes it. But the spiderling is not the only creature out hunting. A frog has spotted the spider and lunges at it. **The spiderling quickly scrambles up its lifeline, but the frog bites off a leg!** How will the little spider survive now?

PLAYING POSSUM

Some spiders trick their enemies by curling their legs under their body and pretending to be dead.

A LEG FOR A LEG

If a spider loses a leg, it will grow a new one at the next molt. Lost legs and other body parts are replaced during molting.

DEADLY STING

Hunting wasps will attack even big wolf spiders. They sting them, then carry them back to a tunnel in the ground. The wasp lays her eggs on the spider and keeps it as food for her grubs.

ENEMIES

Snakes, lizards, frogs, beetles, and ants all eat spiders. Small woodland animals such as shrews hunt them. But their worst enemies are other big spiders ... and people.

23

The spiderling has become a strong young spider now. She probably doesn't remember ballooning into this garden and has forgotten the frog attack. She's got eight fine legs and a web full of food.

It's been a warm summer, and the spider has grown fat on her daily catch of insects. After just a few more meals and molts, she'll look for a safe place to sleep through the winter. Keep an eye out for this garden spider next spring. She's sure to be out spinning big, beautiful webs!

USEFUL ANIMALS

Many people dislike spiders, but they are very useful to us. They eat insects that destroy crops, and mosquitoes that can carry disease.

HOW LONG DO SPIDERS LIVE?

Most spiders live for about a year. Tarantulas live the longest—some females survive for 30 years.

24

DANGEROUS WIDOWS

Most spiders are not dangerous to people. They sting or bite only if somebody annoys them. The black widow is among the few spiders whose poison is harmful to humans. It has a red mark on its body.

HAIRY-SCARY

The Goliath bird-eating spider is the biggest spider in the world. It lives in hot climates. With a leg span of 11 inches (28 cm), it's certainly scary!

ITSY BITSY SPIDER

The smallest spider crawls about in the moss of Samoa. It's about the same size as the period at the end of this sentence.

The female spider
lays eggs.

Spider

A male
and female
spider mate.

The adult spider
spins a web.

The eggs hatch
into spiderlings.

CIRCLE OF LIFE

The spiderlings
balloon away.

The spider molts many
times as it grows.

aphids Small insects that feed on the sap of plants.

book lungs A pair of organs in a spider's abdomen through which it breathes.

bridge line A long silk thread between two twigs that forms the start of a web.

chelicerae The pair of pincers in front of a spider's mouth.

climates Weather conditions usually found in a particular place.

cocoon A silky case spun by water spiders for their eggs.

dragline A silk thread that acts as a safety line.

egg sac The silk bag wrapped around a spider's eggs.

fang A spider's biting mouthpart, through which it can pump poison.

glands Organs in a spider's body that produce important substances such as silk.

grubs The young form of some insects, such as a wasp; another word for larvae.

leg span The distance across an insect's body from the end of one leg to another.

pedipalps A pair of "foot-feelers" alongside a spider's mouth used to hold and crush food; together with a spider's fangs, they act as jaws.

saliva Liquid produced by glands in the mouth.

silk A fine, usually sticky thread spun by spiders.

sperm Fluid produced by male animals that makes a female's eggs grow into babies.

spinnerets Organs in a spider that produce silk threads.

Published by Smart Apple Media

1980 Lookout Drive

North Mankato, Minnesota 56003

Illustration: Desiderio Sanzi

Design: Deb Miner

Library of Congress

Cataloging-in-Publication Data

Morris, Ting.

Spider / by Ting Morris.

p. cm. — (Creepy crawly world)

Summary: An introduction to the physical
characteristics, behavior, and life cycle of
spiders.

ISBN 1-58340-377-9

1. Spiders—Juvenile literature.

[1. Spiders.] I. Morris, Ting. II.Title.

QL458.4M676 2003

595.4'4—dc21   2002044611

Head of Blind-worm. $\frac{1}{2}$

A Book-scorpion (*Chelifer can-croides*). $\frac{5}{1}$

Click-beetle, natural size.

Sinea diadema, one of the *Reduviidæ*. (Line shows natural size.)

a
Cotton-stainer.

Proxys punctulatus.

Hellgrammite (*a*) and Hellgrammite-fly.

The Bait-bug.

Epeiridæ.
a, male, and *b*, fe-male, of *Epeira stel-lata*; *c*, characteristic orb-web of an epeirid (*Epeira strix*).

Parasite of the Beaver (*Platy-psyllus castoris*). (Line shows natural size.)

Rose-beetle (*Cetonia aurata*). Vertical line shows natural size.

Agonoderus dorsalis (Le Conte). Vertical line shows natural size.

The Twig-gir-dler (*Oncideres cingulata*). $\frac{1}{1}$
a, a branch girdled by the beetle.

The Dr
Dragon
(*Drac
eatus.*

Hawthorn-tingis *arcuata*), one of the enlarged about ten ti

Flour-beetle (*Te
litor*). (Line show
size.)

Galeruca notata

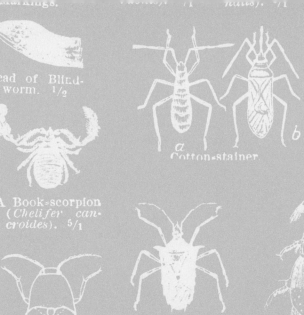

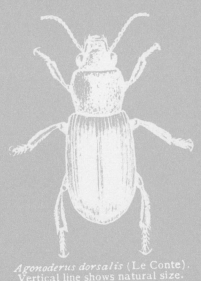
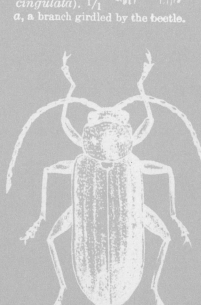

Ground-beetle (*Caloso calidum*), natural size.

Eurygaster alternatus; wings partly open. (Line shows natural size.)

A Species of *Phrynus*, about life-size.

Spiderwort Owlet-moth (*Prodenia flavimedia*). *a*, larva; *b*, wings of moth.

Ephemeridæ.
European May-fly (*Eph-vulgata*) and its sub-larva.

Bombardier-beetle (*Bra-chinus stygicornis*). (Vertical line shows natural size.)

Thighed Metapodius (*Metapo-dius femoratus*).

The Cucujo.

Podisus placidus.
a, enlarged; *b*, natural size.

Libellulidæ.
Development of a dragon-fly, showing the subaquatic larva, emergence from the pupa, and the adult fully winged insect.

A Flea (*Pulex irritans*).
a, puncturing stylets of the proboscis.

A Bristletail (*Lepisma saccharina*). ⁵/₁

Phymata erosa.

Atypus sulzeri. (Vertical line shows natural size.)

Bacon-beetle.

Grape-vine Fidia (*F. viticida*). (Line shows natural size.)

One of